Save, Spend, or Donate?
A Book About Managing Money

written by Nancy Loewen * illustrated by Brian Jensen

Thanks to our advisers for their expertise, research, and advice:

Dr. Joseph Santos
Associate Professor of Economics, Department of Economics
South Dakota State University

Susan Kesselring, M.A., Literacy Educator
Rosemount-Apple Valley-Eagan (Minnesota) School District

PICTURE WINDOW BOOKS
Minneapolis, Minnesota

Managing Editor: Catherine Neitge
Creative Director: Terri Foley
Art Director: Keith Griffin
Editors: Patricia Stockland, Christianne Jones
Designer: Nathan Gassman
Page Production: Picture Window Books
The illustrations in this book were
prepared digitally.

Picture Window Books
5115 Excelsior Boulevard
Suite 232
Minneapolis, MN 55416
877-845-8392
www.picturewindowbooks.com

Printed in the United States of America.

Library of Congress Cataloging-in-Publication Data
Loewen, Nancy, 1964-
Save, spend, or donate? : a book about
managing money / by Nancy Loewen ;
illustrated by Brian Jensen.
p. cm. — (Money matters)
Includes bibliographical references and index.
ISBN 1-4048-0952-X (hardcover)
1. Finance, Personal—Juvenile literature.
2. Children—Finance, Personal—Juvenile
literature. I. Jensen, Brian. II. Title. III. Money matters
(Minneapolis, Minn.)

HG179.L5534 2005
332.024—dc22   2004019187

"We finished our chores. Now it's time for us to collect," said Sam.

"Collect what?" teased Dad.

"Our allowance!" Josie and Sam shouted.

3

Mom got her wallet and handed out dollar bills. Josie and Sam opened their special money boxes and counted their spending money.

"I only have $7," Josie sighed.

"I'm up to $32!" Sam exclaimed. "Can we go to Merry-Mart today? I finally have enough money to buy that remote-control car."

"Sounds good," Dad said.

Some parents don't give allowances. Others give big allowances. Either way, helping around the house is a good thing to do.

Sam and Josie also had envelopes marked "give" and "save." They put part of their money into each envelope.

"These envelopes are getting kind of full," said Sam.

"Let's go to the bank today and make a deposit into your savings account. You should start thinking about where you want to donate your 'give' money," Dad said.

Keeping a lot of cash around is risky. It could be lost or even stolen. A bank is the safest place to keep your money.

7

At the bank drive-through, Mom put the money and deposit slips into the tube. Whoosh! Away it went. When the tube returned, Josie looked at her receipt. She had almost $200.

"Can't I spend some of it?" Josie asked.

"No way," Dad answered. "This is a special account. If you put in a little money every week, it really adds up."

"Saving money a little at a time is a good habit to have," Mom added.

Learning how to save is an important life skill for people of all ages.

9

"What do you save money for?"
Sam asked his parents.

"Some of the money is for when
we retire. We're also saving for
when you kids go to college.
Those are our long-term savings
goals," Dad explained.

"We also set aside money for short-term goals like vacations and presents," Mom said. "And we have money saved for emergencies, too."

Many adults have money taken out of their paychecks. It is sent straight into different savings accounts. This makes it easier to save.

11

At Merry-Mart, Sam and Dad went to the toy aisle. Josie and Mom went to look at clothes.

"Can I get this shirt?" asked Josie. "I'll use my own money. I just need next week's allowance."

"No," Mom said. "Trust me. It isn't fun to have all your money spent before you get it."

"It's not fair," Josie said. "Why does Sam get to buy that toy car today?"

"Because he's been saving for weeks, and you spent your money," Mom said.

"Oh, right," said Josie with a sigh.

People often use a credit card to buy things. This means they borrow money and promise to pay it back later.

13

The family met at the checkout. Sam got out his money. Then he started thinking about how long it took him to save up for the car. Should he really spend all his money today?

Dad seemed to read his mind.

14

"You know, Sam, saving money is great," said Dad. "But it's OK to spend it, too. You've been very responsible and saved your money for something you really want."

"Well ... OK," Sam said and smiled. Dad was right.

Everyone spends differently. Some people find it hard to save, while others find it hard to spend. But both saving and spending are necessary.

On the way home, Dad asked Sam and Josie where they wanted to donate their "give" money. In the past, they gave money to their church and to the area food shelves. They also pledged money for the hunger walk.

That evening, the local news showed an elderly couple's home destroyed by fire. A local bank was setting up a fund to accept donations.

Sam and Josie both had the same idea.

"We've made our decision, Dad," said Josie. "We'll send our 'give' money to that couple."

Giving money to others is an important value in many families.

"You guys are really getting the hang of this money stuff," Dad said.

"Yeah," Sam agreed. "We can take care of ourselves by saving and spending. And we can all help take care of each other by giving to those in need."

Mom smiled. "We've got a couple of smart kids here," she said.

Savings Register

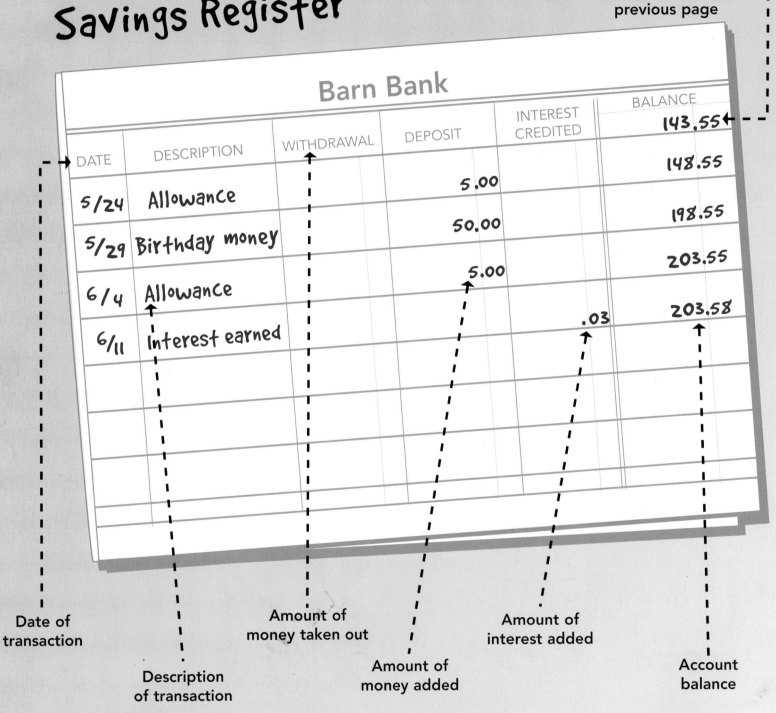

Balance of previous page

Barn Bank

DATE	DESCRIPTION	WITHDRAWAL	DEPOSIT	INTEREST CREDITED	BALANCE
					143.55
					148.55
5/24	Allowance		5.00		
5/29	Birthday money		50.00		198.55
6/4	Allowance		5.00		203.55
6/11	Interest earned			.03	203.58

Date of transaction

Description of transaction

Amount of money taken out

Amount of money added

Amount of interest added

Account balance

22

Fun Facts

- According to a survey by *kidsmoney.org*, kids ages 6 to 8 receive an average allowance of $4 a week. At age 9, they get around $5 a week.

- Every year, people contribute billions of dollars to charities like the Salvation Army, YMCA, American Cancer Society, American Red Cross, Catholic Charities USA, and America's Second Harvest.

- Many Americans have bad spending and saving habits. Experts recommend that people save at least one tenth of their incomes. Most Americans save less than half of that amount. In addition, the average American adult has close to $2,300 in credit card debt.

Glossary

allowance—money given to someone on a regular basis

charity—an organization that helps other people

credit—an agreement to pay for something at a later date

donate—to give money or goods to a charity

interest—money that is paid to people for keeping their money in a bank

pledge—a promise to pay money to a charity

survey—a report in which many people are asked about their beliefs or behavior

transaction—carrying out a business deal

To Learn More

At the Library

Giesecke, Ernestine. *Dollars and Sense: Managing Your Money.* Chicago: Heinemann Library, 2002.

Hall, Margaret. *Your Allowance.* Chicago: Heinemann Library, 2000.

Ziefert, Harriet. *You Can't Buy a Dinosaur with a Dime.* New York: Handprint Books, 2003.

On the Web

FactHound offers a safe, fun way to find Web sites related to this book. All of the sites on FactHound have been researched by our staff.
www.facthound.com

1. Visit the FactHound home page.

2. Enter a search word related to this book, or type in this special code: 140480952X

3. Click on the FETCH IT button.

Your trusty FactHound will fetch the best sites for you!

Look for all of the books in this series:

- Cash, Credit Cards, or Checks: A Book About Payment Methods

- Lemons and Lemonade: A Book About Supply and Demand

- Save, Spend, or Donate? A Book About Managing Money

- Ups and Downs: A Book About the Stock Market

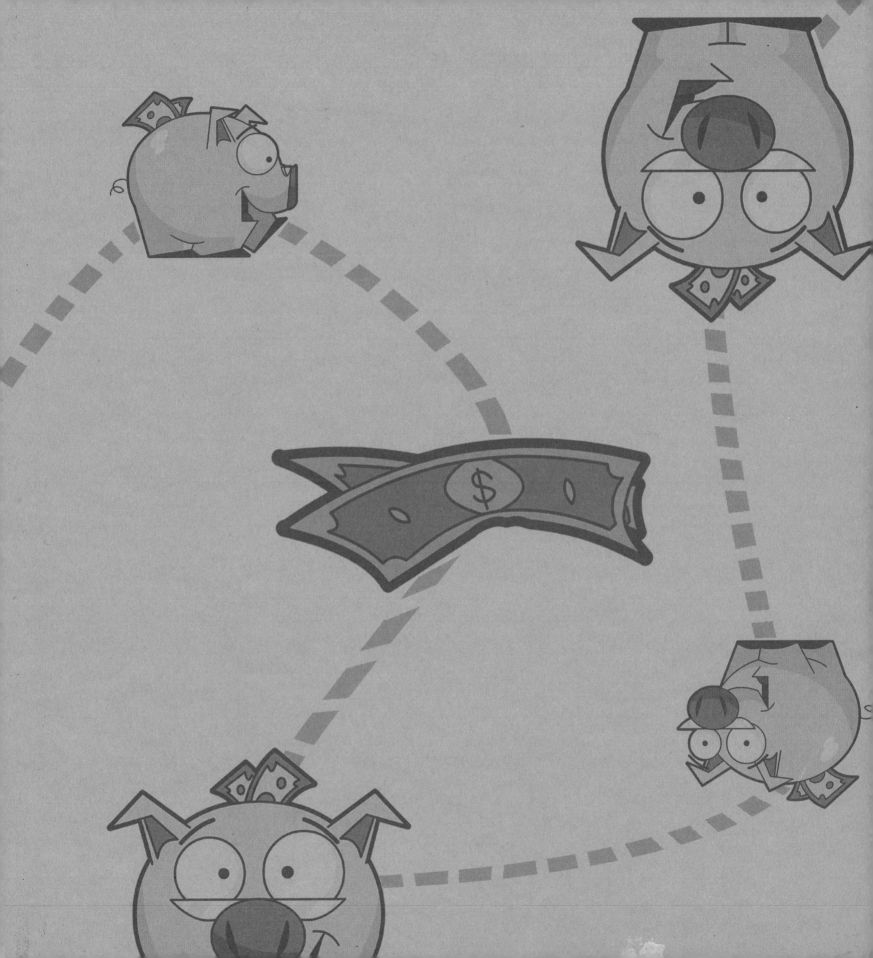